Departure

Departure

Poems

Rosanna Warren

W. W. Norton & Company
New York   London

For information about permission to reproduce selections from this book, write to
Permissions, W. W. Norton & Company, Inc., 500 Fifth Avenue, New York, NY 10110

Manufacturing by Courier Westford
Book design by Lovedog Studio
Production manager: Anna Oler

Library of Congress Cataloging-in-Publication Data
Warren, Rosanna.
Departure : poems / Rosanna Warren.— 1st ed.
p. cm.
ISBN 0-393-05819-0 (hardcover)
I. Title.
PS3573.A7793D47 2003
811'.54—dc21

2003010865

W. W. Norton & Company, Inc.
500 Fifth Avenue, New York, N.Y. 10110
www.wwnorton.com

W. W. Norton & Company Ltd.
Castle House, 75/76 Wells Street, London W1T 3QT

1 2 3 4 5 6 7 8 9 0

For Stephen, who has heard the cicadas singing

in the grove by the River Ilossos

without falling asleep

Contents

III.

IV.

Acknowledgments

Grateful acknowledgment is made to the following journals in which these poems have appeared:

Agni Review: "For Trakl"
Arion: "Turnus"
The Atlantic Monthly: "August Walk"
Drunken Boat: "What Leaves"
Harvard Magazine: "March Snow"
New England Review: "E.W."
The New Republic: " 'Departure,' " "Diversion," "From the
    Notebooks of Anne Verveine I," "Sicily"
The New Yorker: "From the Notebooks of Anne Verveine II,"
    "From the Notebooks of Anne Verveine V," "Hellenistic
    Head," "Island in the Charles," Nightshade," "Travel"
Orion: "L'Oiseau de nuit," "Postscript"
The Paris Review: "Cyprian," "Mud"
Ploughshares: "From the Notebooks of Anne Verveine III"

Raritan: "From the Notebooks of Anne Verveine IV," "Cassandra"
Seneca Review: "Eclogue," "Love Story"
Shenandoah: "Arrival"
Slate: "Day Lilies," "Lake," "Piazza Pilo"
Southwest Review: "North"
Threepenny Review: "Antique"
The Washington Post: "Poetry Reading"
The Yale Review: "Bonfires"

Some of these poems have appeared in the following anthologies: "Bonnard" in *Words for Images: A Gallery of Poems;* "'Departure'" in *Best American Poetry 1998;* "Diversion" in *Best American Poetry 1997* and in *Best American Poetry 1988–1997;* "Eclogue," "What Leaves," "Piazza Pilo," and "Love Story" in *Fine Arts 2001,* Annual Catalogue for The American Academy in Rome; "Moment," "5 P.M.," "Portrait: Marriage" in *Bright Pages;* "Poetry Reading" in *Ecstatic Occasions, Expedient Forms;* "Siderium Exaltatum" in *Another Language of Flowers;* "Turnus" in *Gods and Mortals.*

I am grateful to the American Academy in Rome for a year of peace and freedom in which some of these poems were composed. I thank Boston University for the kindness of allowing me several more leaves than a normal academic schedule permits. Various friends have been scrupulous readers of some of these poems; I am especially grateful to Deborah Tall, David Weiss, David Ferry, Mark Strand, Rika Lesser, Jonathan Aaron, Tom Sleigh, Lloyd Schwartz, and John Peck.

Departure

Cassandra

Don't say that word, comfort

Wherever the splendid sun beats down on sorrow
no one will

hear, but the blind
beggar already totters from chamber to chamber

in the vault, murmuring, embracing urns
that have yet to be filled with

a story that has yet to spark or char the mind

I

———

Hellenistic Head

for Derek Walcott

She's in two worlds, her veil blown half across her face:
hair a dense crown of hyacinth knots, her one
visible eye gone blank. How to make marble drift
like muslin, like sea mist, across a brow?
Under the scarf, the daydream stirs:

                            gash in the morning torn
by the white horse loosed, careening
across two parkway lanes and up the median grass,
thunder made flesh in haunches and arcing neck
as cars streamed by like a doubled Milky Way,
and two small dark figures, arms upraised,
jostled along the highway shoulder, swinging rope.
We were children, nestled by speed into the backseat
of our speeding car. The horse was a comet,
mane and tail igniting a drizzled day.

And we are gone in the hurtling car, my brother and I,
forty years gone in that torrent of fumes and chrome
that snatched away childhood house and barn and the

                                hummocky field,
slow-syrup hours of Sunday afternoons
with creaky floorboards and spiders curled in the knotholes of

                                          beams,
and the demigods who drove the car and admonished us
and conversed unknowably in the sanctum of the front seat.

The horse's eyes bulged yogurt-white from bloody rims,
big as croquet balls and veiny with panic,
but sparked, too, with glee
to see his world so streamingly wide and fast.
He was likely, it was clear, to be horribly hurt.
He was likely to kill people.
                              In the Hellenistic head,
half the face freezes in the fully empty gaze.
The other half is stone that turns into wind.

Arrival

(Poseidon, *Iliad* XIII)

That's how a god descends from a mountain peak
in Samothrace: startled attention stirs him, then
three strides vault him down to the plain as oak roots shake
and boulders lurch from the cliff face, vomiting down

its loosened jaw of scree: that's how a god descends,
the fourth stride thunders him into his harbor pool
at Aigai where, gold in the weedy depths, his palace bends
the sun beams: golden the armor he buckles, all

sun-hammered glint and gleam the bridles he fastens
on golden-maned horses, his whip a gold parabola in foam,
chariot a churning glare on a wave that glistens:
that's how a god arrives, how grief will come

any day, any ordinary hour, when all we see
is a peculiar, shivering brilliance in the air
like a premonition of migraine; and no one can see
later, how in such a flash, the dark came there.

Cyprian

(Phi Beta Kappa Poem, Yale 2000)

We could almost see her
where she is said to have risen in the bay
from sea foam and the blood of Ouranos' sliced genitals
tossed out of heaven.

We could almost see
how she must have sat on the long arm of rock
that half-cradled the bay
and how she combed seaweed out of her hair with a scallop shell

before rising in a commotion of salt light and doves' wings
to terrorize the earth.
Squinting, we could almost believe
as we could almost see

inland, at Paphos, her temple erect
on the ruined marble floor paving
amid column chunks and cringing olive trees
as the horizon trembled in haze

and distant mountains tried in their softness to resemble the
female body.
But it was inside
that shed of a museum across the spongy road, our eyes
maladjusted to dimness, that

she appeared, I think: if it is in
the sudden intake of breath, the fluttered pulse, that she registers:
not as one would have imagined,
no body at all, no womanliness,

not Greek, not even human as a god should be,
but that uncarven black vertical basalt thrust
into consciousness
throbbed in the room alone,

just a rock
on a pedestal, a terrible rock
they worshipped epochs ago before the Greeks
gave her a name a story a shape:

a rock in the dark for which we had paid in Cypriot coins,
for which we still clutched
small paper tickets, damp in our palms.
When I have fought you

most, when we have lain
separate in the puzzle of sheets
until dawn flushed away clots of night, and still we lay apart:
she was there, she presided—

she of the many names:
sea-goddess; foam-goddess; heavenly
Ourania crowned, braceleted and beringed in gold and gems;
Melaina the black one; Skotia, dark one;

Killer of Men; Gravedigger; She-Upon-the-Graves;
Pasiphaessa the Far-Shining;
and she to whom we sacrificed,
Aphrodite Apostrophia,

She Who Turns Herself Away.

Poetry Reading

manibus date lilia plenis (Aeneid VI)

It is a promise they hold in their hands.
Feathers waver in the ghostly crests.
Rome is an iron glint in the eyes,
a twitch at sword hilt. Down the long avenue
through silted shadow and pale leaking light
stalks the future. Power,
whispers the father, power bounded
only by the edge of earth, the rim of heaven.
The arts of peace, the rule of law:
the Capitol, aqueducts, legions, circuses.
Disorder chained in the temple. Abundant calm.
In such love you have given yourself.

But who is that young one, pallid
in armor with darkened brow
and night coming on at his heels,
scent of crushed lilies, a bruise—

Here the reading breaks off.
The emperor's sister falls into hysterical tears,
patrons and literati disband.
Servants clear away wine-cups, platters of cake.

And Aeneas climbs back into daylight
through the gate of false dreams.

Turnus

(*Aeneid* XII)

for Michael Putnam

Not lion, not wind, not fire, not sacrificial
bull, not in strength and sinew god-
like, nor even as stag, Silvia's gentle
one, tame, tower-antlered, awash in the sweet blood

of his groin where the Trojan arrow struck—
no beast, no simile, Turnus, but a man alone
when your knees buckle and you look back
at the ashen city, the girl with her eyes cast down,

away. You've crashed to your side, the spear
has whispered its only message through the air.
And when you speak, and He seems inclined to hear,
it's the woods that reply, the shadowed hilltops near

and farther, and what they speak is a groan
for a lost world, for leaflight, the childhood grove
where the small stream stammered its rhymes in amber and
                                        green.

And if He pauses? If His sword hovers above

your chest? Here's where you tear a hole in the poem,
a hole in the mind, here's where the russet glare
of ships aflame and the pyre and the amethyst gleam
from the boy's sword belt rise and roil in a blur.

We are trapped in meanings that circulate like blood.
The sword descends. And He who kills you is not
a myth, nor a city. His eyes searching yours could
be a lover's eyes. It was love He fought.

"Departure"

(from Max Beckmann and Guido Guinizelli)

"I can only speak to people who—"

Unspeaking, unspoken, the full-breasted woman
tied to a dead man upside down

stands center stage with a lamp in her hand,
sheds kerosene glow on the marching band.

That's Cupid, the dark dwarf who tightens her rope;
this is art, this is love, that's the classical shape

of proscenium arch. This is Germany, May '32.
"—can only speak to people who

already carry, consciously or unconsciously, within them—"

You want to buy that center panel, Lilly, but
you can't have that alone

There will always be, on one side, a man bound to a column
with both hands chopped off; there will always be
a still life with hand grenade grapes and a woman kneeling
before an executioner who swings a bag of iron fish

Love always shelters in the gentle heart

And you will always—won't you?—find yourself groping
in a dark stairwell ill-lit by that feeble, dangerous lamp
while you drag along, strapped to you, the corpse of all your
                                                    errors,
and the drum throbs and shudders like a titanic heart

Love's fire is kindled in the gentle heart
as light kindles in a precious gem

And there's another romance, in which the woman
and man are strapped to each other alive, but head to feet,
                                    on a giant fish
and each holds in hand the ritual mask of the other
as they hurtle downward toward a brilliant, engulfing ocean

as the star beam strikes the water
but the sky keeps the star and all its fire

which is generally known as love. No, you can't
buy the central panel alone, with the king and queen
joyous and powerful in their open boat, the baby bespeaking
freedom
and the net full of fish flashing in blessed abundance

"—who already carry, consciously or unconsciously, within them
a similar metaphysical code."

because the oarsman is blindfolded
because the crowned fisherman has his back to us
because that open boat
has not set sail
from our shores
nor will it, while we are alive.

Mud

(for John Walker)

It's not as simple as rhyming "mud" and "blood"
        as Owen did and does ("I, too, saw God through mud")
        in his "Apologia."
Or feces and "fecit" which is
        a kind of rhyme as in
        "Walker fecit," which he

did and does through
        mud, bruised flesh, pigment, glossy
        oil pressed from memory's trench:
"God" rhymes of course with
        everything. It's not enough
        to spread damp clay ("Was it for this

the clay grew tall?") across canvas: he can't
        bury fathers, uncles,
        sons, they keep
sprouting, worms their words ("Men went
        to Catraeth as day
        dawned"): Our words, his

words: Aneirin, Jones, a seethe on
        the surface we cannot
        possess. The dead belong
to no one, live their own
        maggoty life observed
        by the small, sheep-skulled soldier;

by the father who clambers out of the painter's skull;
        by the easel which wants
        to be lantern and cross.
The Somme? July 1, 1916: men went, men
        want: all those men marched
        which century? Sixth? The

Welsh at Catraeth, three hundred dead: a sum:
        a song. Whose ribcage
        gapes? Whose numbers ooze
in the ditch of years? This painter comes
        too late. He hoists
        his loops of pods upon

a firmament of mud, he hangs dark swags
        of script and
        sacrament. (A
duchess approves. She likes chiaro-
        scuro in love and
        war). The painter has brought

a necklace—no, a rosary—of human
       kidneys, slick
       and soiled. It is
not as easy as rhyming "mud"
       and "blood." The words belong
       to no one. (Not that we

wanted. Not that we wanted to know.)

A Questionnaire for Bernard Chaet

Can a scar emit light?

Can objects slide off the curved surface of the earth?

Can the sea rise up like a serene, implacable wall of mother-
of-pearl?

    (Can we see through that wall?)

Can a sword of sunlight crack rocks?

Can a rainstorm form an isosceles triangle?

Can a garden roll up into a bristling globe?

    (Was that the first garden?)

Have we lost the sky, looking down?

Were we ever safe here?

Do you find, in fracture, a motive for praise?

Do you remember a promise of peace?

    (Have you signed your name?)

II

———————————

Island in the Charles

"By being scholar first of that new night"

(CRASHAW)

Taking the well-worn path in the mind though dusk encroaches
upon the mind, taking back alleys careful step by step
past parked cars and trash containers, three blocks to the
                concrete ramp
of the footbridge spanning the highway with its rivering,
                four-lane
unstaunchable traffic, treading on shadow and slant broken light

my mother finds her way. By beer bottles, over smeared
Trojans, across leafmuck, she follows the track, clutching her
jacket close. The footbridge lofts her over the flashing cars
and sets her down, gently, among trees, where she is a child
in the weave of boughs, and leafshapes plait the breeze.

She fingers silver-green blades of the crack willow, she tests
                dark grooves
of crack willow bark. The tree has a secret. Its branches pour
themselves back toward earth, and my mother pauses, dredging
                a breath
up out of her sluggish lungs. The blade leaves scratch
her fingertips, the corrugated bark

releases a privacy darker than cataract veils.
But slashed and ribboned, glimpsed through fronds,
the river hauls its cargo of argent light
and she advances, past basswood and crab apple clumps
along the tarmac where cyclists, joggers, rollerbladers

entranced in their varying orbits swoop
around her progress. With method, she reaches her bench,
she stations there. She sits columnular, fastened
to her difficult breath, and faces the river in late afternoon.
Behind her, voices. Before her, the current casts its glimmering

seine to a shore so distant no boundary scars
her retina, and only occasional sculls or sailboats flick
across her vision as quickened, condensing light.
There she sits, poised, while the fluent transitive Charles
draws off to the harbor and, farther, to the unseen sea

until evening settles, and takes her in its arms.

E.W.

Your purpled, parchment forearm
lodges an IV needle and valve;
your chest sprouts EKG wires;
your counts and pulses swarm

in tendrils over your head
on a gemmed screen: oxygen,
heart rate, lung power, temp
root you to the bed—

Magna Mater, querulous, frail,
turned numerological vine
whose every brilliant surge
convolutes the tale,

translates you to a life
shining beyond our own:
Come back to the world
we know the texture of—

demand your glasses back,
struggle into your clothes,
lean on me as you walk
into the summer dark

where you'll find once more your breath
and scold the wasted night.
Above us, satellites vastly wink.
Laugh. Come forth.

Diversion

Go, I say to myself, tired of my notebooks and my reluctant pen,
go water the newly transplanted sorrel and dill,
spriggy yet in their new humus and larger clay pots;
water artemisia, salvia, centaurea
which are classical, perennial, and have promised to spread
                                        their nimbus
of violet and silver through our patchy backyard
for summers to come, from poor soil.
Then I'll return indoors to the words copied
on the yellow legal pad,

her words
which I cannot shape,
which sentence me:

"There are things I prefer
        to forget—"
                (what things?) "Just,

things—" "Darling, I can't
        locate myself—" "Where
            are *you?*"

And if she, in her compassion, forgets
or doesn't know, I will perennially remember,
how I erase these messages
I later transcribe: one punch
of one button on the answering machine—

and how, with cruel
helpfulness
I have asked:

"Don't you remember?"

restoring to her a garden of incident
which she cannot keep, water, or tend,
and which will die, soon, from her ministrations.

L'Oiseau de nuit

I wanted to read to you
    Colette's story about her mother calling
and calling her children in
    the lush, half-ruined garden in Burgundy
while the children hid in pine
    trees and the hay loft and roamed in swamp and field:

so we sat at the scarred oak
    table Pa had glued, pegged, sanded and varnished
forty-odd years earlier,
    and let Colette's wisteria seize on us
(*la glycine centenaire,*
    she called it) as it had seized and wrenched the old

iron garden gate in that
    story where everything tumbles but resists—
gate, stone wall, sagging massive
    lilac bush, the children bruised, scratched, bleeding but
free—we sat in the after-
    -noon, and her words, *glycine, buanderie, pourpre,*

led us. Two years ago you
        still could follow prose. Colette's mother kept on
calling as evening fell
        in that garden, "Where are the children?" Their one
sin, says Colette, was silence.
        Her mother's arms were flour-whitened; she shook

blood-stained butcher paper to
        lure her cats as she called; when she knew she was
dying, she ordered a robe
        for burial—long, hooded, lace-collared—(that
is not in the story) and
        wrote her daughter, "To think I could die without

seeing you again." We drank
        tea, we looked up *buanderie* (washhouse), we
closed the book leaving Colette's
        mother still crying, *"Où sont les enfants?"* and
made our sort of peace with dusk
        as it gathered in the arbor vitae hedge:

I peeled the carrots, you had
        your glass of wine, my children came tramping in—
noisy, not bleeding, hungry—
        and Colette dancing "L'Oiseau de nuit" at Le
Bataclan Club did not and did
        not visit Sido (her mother) whose heart lapsed

and persistently lapsed yet
  lurched along; nor did you understand when I
tried the garden story a-
  -gain this spring. Never mind. At least we sat to-
-gether as yet another
  twilight sifted down and softened our voices,

and, in late August, Colette
  did leave lover, theater, writing desk and cats,
"three whole days," for Sido, whose
  heart, three weeks later, halted flat. No daughter
at her funeral, nor did
  Colette wear black. Those children are still roaming

loose, wild, hurting themselves, and
  I sit here stubbornly miles from you in my
own garden by the arbor
  vitae wrenched wide open by last winter's snow,
remembering Colette, and
  once again hold a book up between us: "The

house and garden still live, I
  know, but for what, if their magic is gone, if
the secret is lost which o-
  -pened—sunlight, odors, harmony of trees and birds,
murmur of voices now quelled
  by death—a world which I no longer deserve?"

Simile

As when her friend, the crack Austrian skier, in the story
she often told us, had to face
his first Olympic ski jump and, from
the starting ramp over the chute that plunged
so vertiginously its bottom lip
disappeared from view, gazed
on a horizon of Alps that swam and dandled around him
like toy boats in a bathtub, and he could not
for all his iron determination,
training and courage
ungrip his fingers from the railings of the starting gate, so that
his teammates had to join in prying
up, finger by finger, his hands
to free him, so

facing death, my
mother gripped the bedrails but still
stared straight ahead—and
who was it, finally,
who loosened
her hands?

Postscript

The one who jackhammered up the surface of the morning
    and stacked it in chunks by the side of the road—
The one who yanked the bandage off the sky
    so it bled again, there, in the cleft between the trees—
The smiling one who held the morphine vial and murmured
    "There, there" (I think she was the angel of death)—

*

Over the black pond spreads a film of ice
like glaucoma, but water
wells out beyond ice, beyond
stones, beyond weed tufts: o new
season gleaming darkly from half-frozen mud
you reflect
nothing—

    Underfoot,
oak leaves lie tender, bleached and damp,
palms upward—

Overhead, cloud shreds
flutter on branch tips in
a tatterdemalion sky

*

Yes, he said, legs braced wide apart,
I can make words jump through hoops, stand on one paw,
spin their tails in the air

It's a matter of training

It's a profession
if not a faith

                              *

"I told the daughter it was
time to call in Hospice—"

"I *am* 'the daughter'—"

                              *

And in her room
the rented hospital bed, empty, half-
stripped (who will sleep now
in those sheets?); telephone
silent; toothbrush and dentures
a still life on the faux-marble washbasin;
her washcloth slowly stiffening on the towel rack;
shopping lists, buttons, passport, loose keys
lying in pharaonic darkness at the backs of drawers
                              are in for a

long wait:

                                        as are the
blank future day slots on her calendar
lying sidewise on her desk

                    *

          My days are swifter than a weaver's shuttle

So she floated in the red
        armchair, so her tongue couldn't find
its lair in her mouth:

so her ankles swelled, so
        each breath snared and hauled
up a groan from its burrow of dark:

so she leaned forward, held my
        hand, and said,"Your hands
are cold—" And: "Please—please—"

          O remember that my life is wind

We are Greek figures in a *bas
        relief,* two women leaning toward
each other across a

void: not marble but
        light draws us
together, cuts us apart, incises

our profiles against
      this night that repeats
forever, will perish with each

breath: not marble
      can hold in mind
the shape of vanishing

        As the cloud is consumed and vanisheth away

*

"Ma, is breathing hard for you?"
"No; thinking is."

           And, shifting in her chair:

"Let me just see—if I can see—
      how to ease things a little—if
         anything can—

Time to break this off—

I can't see—I can't see what to do—"

*

In the grove of white pines, by the granite ledge,
a ring of soot-black stones. Charred sticks. Ashes.
Broken glass glints like sequins in the tamped-down dirt.
Pine needles—faded russet—have drifted across the clearing
which is small, hidden away, high off the main trail.
We stand here, the dog and I, as if abashed
at having broken into someone's house.
Someone, however, who moved away long ago.
Silence absorbs us. Faintly, the breeze
fingers bare branches to which spring has not yet occurred.
Then a mourning dove gives a tentative call
trying out his voice upon our motionlessness
until he falters, releasing us from the spell,
and we make our way back through the woods, toward the
                                            homeward path.

So have whole tribes
passed from the memory of earth.

Day Lilies

For six days, full-throated, they praised
the light with speckled tongues and blare
    of silence by the porch stair:
honor guard with blazons and trumpets raised
still heralding the steps of those
    who have not for years walked here
    but who once, pausing, chose

this slope for a throng of lilies:
and hacked with mattock, pitching stones
    and clods aside to tamp dense
clumps of bog-soil for new roots to seize.
So lilies tongued the brassy air
    and cast it back in the sun's
    wide hearing. So, the pair

who planted the bulbs stood and heard
that clarion silence. We've heard it,
    standing here toward sunset
as those gaping, burnished corollas poured
their flourish. But the petals have
    shrivelled, from each crumpled knot
    droops a tangle of rough

notes shrunk to a caul of music.
Extend your palms: you could as well
        cup sunbeams as pour brim-full
again those absent flowers, or touch the quick
arms of those who bent here, trowel in
        hand, and scraped and sifted soil
        held in a bed of stone.

Siderium Exaltatum

(Starry Venusweed)

for Dorothea Tanning

Tapering to char
the wicks seek consummation
beyond the body:
one roused from ovaries of light,
one from a dying star.

III

Intimate Letters

The last string quartet

(Leoš Janáček and Kamila Stösslová)

She reads romances, she spells poorly, she's full-breasted,
broad in the beam, matron in a cloche hat,
bulky knee-length skirt, apron, thick calves, white stockings,
Mary Janes.

Her heels go click click on the pavement.
She has those dark Gypsy eyes and the wide laugh.
He loves it when she tosses her head like that.
And here she is in long skirt and embroidered blouse, posing
by her dwarf ornamental orange tree on the balcony:
high pale forehead, stacked dark hair, heavy jaw, bust cleaving
forward like a prow.
And here she is on holiday with her husband the businessman
the perpetual traveller
with the commanding walk and striped tie and blunt mustache.

"Two decidedly Jewish types," writes Zdenka Janáčková, J's wife:

they send her, in the last year of the war,
bread, butter, eggs, semolina flour, geese
from the husband's military contacts.

*

"My dear dark dove," J calls Kamila, "My little one."

*

He has taken dictation from every fountain in Hukvaldy,
where he was born to endless mumbled rosaries of water.
He notes the gush and prattle of the Fox's Well
as the beech tree flashes its sleight of leaf, and fox kits hide in
                                        the rocks;
the public fountain, "a fine of ten crowns
on those who fail to replace the cover":
and when the cover is replaced
the fountain closes her eyes;
the castle fountain, handsome, broad and brimming, but
                                    scuttled into pipes
for manor farm, brewery and slaughterhouse
where the stream blurts out in blood;
and the little well hidden through tall grass at Kazničov,
springing up through the roots of three lime trees, "Helisov's
                                        Well,"
chants the little girl, and he notes that too, the quavering fall
of the name; and watches water bugs skitter
and green moss, darkling, at the bottom, and shards of sky.

*

Bread, butter, eggs, semolina flour, geese.
Kamila knows nothing of music, she worries about her dress
for the première of *Jenůfa* in Vienna.
She has two little boys, Rudi and Otto.
Otto the baby swims on her hand
and she leans over him, soft as night, one eyebrow tilted up
as at a dream of which she is hardly aware.

*

"She was of medium height, dark, curly-haired like a Gypsy
woman,"
writes Zdenka, "with great, black bulging eyes.
The voice was unpleasant, shrill."

*

—That once again he saw "her raven hair, all loose,"
and she was barefoot in the house
and she climbed a ladder to pick apricots from the tree
and she refused the gift of the knitted silver bag
"And your eye has a strange depth, it's so deep it doesn't shine."

*

Night leans hugely.
He sleeps alone, in his study, upstairs at the Organ School.
Zdenka sleeps in their villa across the yard.

*

He who had scrawled
on his cuffs, on envelope scraps, on market paper, in his little pad,
robins' trills, girls' chatter at the railway station,

fox bark, thrush whistle, hen cackle,
kitten mew, bee hum, "the chord of stalagmites covered with
                                    hoarfrost,"
the airy, bell-like patter of fountain spray,

    scored
    in a notebook
    years before Kamila
    in a notebook
    2 A.M. 24 February 1903

    his daughter's dying
    words—
    Olga—
    dying, age 21—
    in a notebook—

"Now I remember that I'm supposed to die"
(a little string of quarter notes, B and middle C)—
"What walks we took on the corso"—"We
should say so much—"

He tells her,
"You are the most beautiful among them," and she smiles,
in his notebook she smiles.
And, down to a G,

"Something gets lost so well, no one can find it."

In a notebook—
2:45 A.M. 25 February 1903, Olga,
her light hair spread across the pillow,

sighs

"A-y-a," two drawn out B's, scrupulously noted by her father,
and in the margin,

"God be with you, my soul."

*

What can be assimilated into song?

*

The rivers of Lachia: the River Lubina
falls from a ridge of the Radhošť Mountain
into an abyss, to seethe of silver, crash of dark;
the Ondřejnice dabbles through the village of Měrkovice,
past mossy banks, shallow, beery-blonde, tepid, where goslings
                                     swim

dunking for weeds and bugs; and the River Ostravice
is the color of steel, and smites the wrist with cold:

and all the Lachian rivers run
through cello depths, horn hurtle, foam-spray of glockenspiel,
clash of cymbals at the smoky inn
where Sofie Harabisová flies from arm to arm
in the glare, smoke, sweat and stamp of feet:

"Where is the poet Šťastný or Professor Batěk or Mrs. Marie
                                  Jungova now?
Gone, all gone, those who took part
that wild summer night, forty-five years ago!"

*

Kamila reads romances.

"There's no love just innocent
friendship. My husband's
away all the time he's always
got things to do."

*

"Your raven hair—
I write these lines so they'll be read, and yet unread
because unanswered.
So it's like a stone falling into water—"

"You're the star I look for in evening—"
"I was your shadow—"
"Even thoughts become flesh—"

in the fountain bubbling up among the lime tree roots,
mumbling its prayers over and over, tonguing the stones.

*

Now after the war, no need
for bread, butter, eggs, semolina flour, geese delivered
by special connection
and Czechoslovakia is free in the *Sinfonietta,* in the razzle of
brass:

"I'm really
an ordinary woman Your heart would stop
aching if you saw me more."

There's Rudi, there's Otto,
and her husband always dealing in his antiques.

No we cannot attend the première in Prague no we cannot.
Now after the war.

For that cold: boil three onions with marjoram and lemon peel
and drink it like tea with sugar.

Your raven hair.
I was your shadow, when you reached for the apricots.

*

Gut scrapings: the bow scrapes sunlight from that summer
                              day at the spa at Luhačovice
where she sat on the grass "like an exhausted little bird":

"Dear Madam, Accept these few roses as a token"

where she sat on the grass, scrape sunlight
from the inner petals, scrape the dark from
her pupil, so deep it doesn't shine.

Madam:

"Silence goes to sleep under every tree."
Under the tilt of her shadowed brow.
His baby son died those years ago

                              and Olga's hair
spreads wide across the pillow where she sighs.

He sleeps alone
it's like a stone
falling.

Lullaby,
bee swarms,
gut scraping, fracture, a waltz
falters, the schmaltzy tune with raven hair
whispers, breaks off, and the hand she lets him
touch, for the first time, she does not draw away
the first time, "your little hand,"
in eleven years, under the linden boughs.

"That dark Jewess," writes Zdenka, "I rather
liked her at first, but I held my position.
You know how artists are. They have to be
handled. I would not

let him go."

*

"These letters were written in fire."

Zdenka must
        understand:
                Kamila is

the Gypsy girl, Káťa Kabanová, the Vixen, Aljeja,
the little hidden well by the lime trees at Kazničov,
the military fanfare on the promenade,
trumpet, oboe, piccolo squeal
when the Austrians march out, the Empire crashes, and the
country is,
like the high-wire flute notes, finally, free.

Zdenka must acknowledge this:
These letters
were written in fire.

*

By now Kamila's boys have been stuffed into trousers, stiff
collars, and neckties.
They've grown leggy, their faces are plump.
It's a question of tempi slightly retarded, a vertigo
the viola suffers, following the violins.
Silence goes to sleep under every tree.
The cello drags
gusts of confetti, repetition, emotion is all

repetition

pulled by twisted horsehair
out of gut.

My dear dark dove, a form of mourning,
that too is a form
of repetition.

Why don't you write.

So when, those last days, she has come
at last, with little Otto, respectably
to visit the upstairs room he has built and furnished for her
in his summer cottage in Hukvaldy,

furnished according to his dream—
"I want to have the painting of those two cherubs, a writing
                                            desk, a communal table,
a comfortable bed, perhaps of brass, a wardrobe with mirrored
                                            doors, a marble wash-stand,
and four chairs, each from a different part of the world—"

     (the question is, what can be assimilated
     into song)

she peels oranges, makes tea,
they shop in the market and play and walk
and August 8, on the walk up the Babí hůra Hill, Otto gets lost
                                    in the woods and ravines—

Something gets lost so well, no one can find it—

and Leoš seeks and seeks the child in drenching rain
as if searching for his own
son
in the woods and ravines
under the wing of her darkly tilting brow

and returns
fevered.

In a notebook no one writes, no one scores his cough.
10 August 1928 J consents to go
to the hospital in Ostrava

pneumonia—deterioration—sedative

    What walks we took on the corso
        Something gets lost so well
    So it's like a stone

    Silence goes to sleep under every tree
        I was your shadow
    I burned your letters but I keep

                                  the ash

No one scored the sleep rattle in Ostrava
12 August 10 A.M. Sunday Kamila at his side,

a heavy woman who spells poorly, broad in the beam,
with thick knees and white stockings,
who reads romances,
who will die of cancer
seven years later
at 43
and be buried in the Jewish cemetery in Písek.

> "And I kissed you
> And you are sitting beside me and I am happy and at peace.
> In such a way do the days pass for the angels."

No one scored the sleep rattle Sunday 12 August.
Only then, by his order,

Zdenka
is told
and arrives by train.

                    These letters were written in fire.

From the Notebooks of Anne Verveine

I.

When his dogs leapt on Actaeon, he
cried (did he cry out?)—He flung

his arm to command, they tore his hand
from the wrist stump, tore

guts from his belly through the tunic, ripped
the cry from his throat.

That's how we know a god, when the facts
leap at the tenderest innards, and we know

the god is what we can't change. You
stood over me as I woke, I opened my eyes, I saw

that I'd seen and that it was too
late: the seeing

of you in the doorway with weak electric light
fanning behind you in the hall, and my room and narrow pallet
                                    steeped in shadow

were what I couldn't change, and distantly
I wanted you, and, as distantly,

I heard the dogs, baying.

II.

And yet the fountain spends itself, and it is
in the clear

light of its losing that we seem
to take delight:

you dipped your hand in its running braid
to sprinkle my forehead, my lips.

Garden deities observed us: three nymphs
with moss staining their haunches, a pug-nosed faun.

The wound in water closed
perfectly around your gesture, erasing it,

so that only the glimmer, swiftly
drying, on my face recalled

our interruption
of the faultless, cold, passionate, perpetual

idea of the stream's descent—
which, unlike ours, would always be renewed.

III.

I kissed a flame, what did I expect.

Those days, you painted in fire. Tangerine, gold:
one would have had to be a pilgrim to walk
through that wall of molten glass.

And purification
could be conceived, if not
attained, only after many years,

in autumn, in a fire greater than yours,
though menstrual blood still tinged the threshold
and our ex-votos were sordid—scraps of blistered flesh

taped to kitsch prayer cards—and neither of us knew
the object of this exercise, except
having, inadvertently, each of us, burned

we recognized the smell
of wood smoke, the slow swirl
flakes of wood ash make in heavy air;

and we were ready, each in a private way, to make
the gifts the season required.
Mine was the scene

of my young self in your arms,
eyes in your eyes, clutched in the effort
to give each other away—when I glimpsed

behind your pleasure, fear; behind
fear, anger; and knew
in a bolt some gifts

conceal a greater gift.
I have kept it. Now I am ready to give it back
into darker flame

in this season of goldenrod, the ardent weed,
and Queen Anne's lace in its mantilla of ash.
And yet, how lumpishly, how stupidly I stand.

How much that is human will never burn.

IV.

And if you should answer?
I listened, years before I knew you, to the whine
of wind through the high stony pastures above my childhood
                                                    village;

I breathed lavender and thyme and burned my bare legs
on nettles, scraped them on thistles, and rubbed
the sore skin till it reddened all the more. When we

walked the uplands together, you burned your hand
and I kissed the crimsoning nettle-rash. "We are the Lords of
                                                    need,"
you said Hafiz said,

and I believed you, and we were.
In the rugs of your country, carmine is crushed
from insects, cochineal; saffron gold

is boiled from crocus stamens; and indigo
of heaven and fountain pools is soaked, hours upon hours,
from indigo leaves. "Like the angel Harut,"

you said, "We are in the calamity of love-desire."
The angel is chained by neck and knees, head down, in the pit
                                                    of Babel
for falling in love. Your carpets

told a different story: scarlet and saffron
blush as in Paradise, and God reveals himself
in wine, flame, tulips, and the light in a mortal eye.

All night you held me, sleepless, on my childhood cot in the
                                                    stone house;
all night the wind seethed through crags and twisted olive trees,
high on the scents of thyme and goat droppings. "All night,"

Hafiz sang, "I hope the breeze of dawn will cherish the lovers."
But the breeze of dawn is the angel of death.
You are in your far landscape now, I am in mine:

the wind complains and I can't understand the words.
And if you should answer?
You, ten years away, in a different wind.

"We are in the calamity," Hafiz sang. "But tell the tale
of the minstrel and of wine, and leave time alone. Time
is a mystery no skill will solve." We should

thread words like pearls, you said, and the grateful sky
would scatter the Pleiades upon us
though we couldn't see, and that was long ago.

V.

The carpet is not a story. It is a place,
garden of crisscrossed pathways, labyrinth,
fountain, pool, and stream.

As though the fabric had ripped at the vanishing point
at the top of the street
of ashen façades and slate-sloped roofs, you stepped

through the gap, out of your own world.
I had already lost my world.
We met in a torn design

which we tore further, pulling the tall warp,
thread wrapped tightly around our fingers until it bit the flesh
and the rue de Lille unravelled.

I know about design: it's my job,
arranging other people's letters in star charts
that phosphoresce in the dark between the closed covers of
books.

You knew about design from the holes
blown through your country.
We spoke in a language of no country on earth.

You moved slowly, in shadow, teaching the shadows
to echo my name. You ripped my shirt at the neck.
Was it The Beloved I held, holding you?

Down the middle of the carpet the river
weaves a thousand gray glimmers into the deeper green.
The river knows about mourning; that's its job.

How many years has it practiced? With such fleet fingers. A man
woke me at dawn this morning, sobbing and cursing in the street,
reeling from sidewalk to gutter and back again.

On my long gray street, the rue de Lille, where I still live.

IV

5 P.M.

Down Fairview, you could pluck the spine of reflected streetlight
from asphalt.

The afternoon's flesh lies loosely, likely to slip.
Rose of Sharon with its maimed hands, privet, dead morning
                                        glory, rhododendron

have delivered their secrets
to January rain, to the drench of early dark,

to the long-fingered interrogations of a season that prayed for
                                        snow
and was disappointed. Therefore it dissolves

tree knots, aluminum siding, cement embankments, bevelled
                                        porch columns
into streaming sheets, gutter whorls, cataracts

down alley stairs; therefore it loosens roots
of azaleas defunct in ornamental gray pressed-stone garlanded
                                        pots

and floods the sarcophagi; therefore the ex-Presbyterian
                                        fieldstone church
on the corner of Fairview and South

announces "The Boston School of Modern Languages"
in an eddy of street torrents and regurgitating storm drains

and foists its mute megaphone clamped to a chimney pot
against the gargled sky.

Travel

43,000 feet below us
New England is a dun, scuffed, moulting carpet
with here and there a nick of light, as from broken glass.

Clouds trail across it like strands of grandmotherly hair.
With grave and steadfast shudders
we lunge through massive air.
We are flying south.

The inner Plexiglas windowpane,
chill to my fingertip, chill to my cheek,
has been incised by a human hand with zigzag and long cedilla.
The outer pane bears an ideograph of frost
resembling, now an intricate map of suburban roads and
                                                    driveways,
now a star.
                On the wing, the paint
blisters in gunmetal eczema.

Unbolted, my heart
is a missile
heading, in every sense, in the wrong direction.

Moment

When you turned to me—you in bed, still sleepwarm, against
                                        the pillows,
I across the room, skirt zipped, stockings on—
and you asked, so quietly,

"Was that a truthful answer?"

and outside our narrow third-storey window
the Norway maple was poking odd thumbs into the sky
and a skim milk early morning light leaked down the street,
down front porch steps, around grimed collars of snowbanks,
and the oval Victorian mirror of my dresser
reflected all that, with odd angles of rooflines, gutters, chimneys
                            jutting into its peripheral vision,

your question cut
like a knife so sharpened it
 slices clean and the surprised flesh doesn't know for a moment
                                how to bleed,

and I answered, after a pause
in which the strangeness felt like a form of love,

"No."

Nightshade

Suddenly, looking once more at the Japanese elm, I saw
that you do not exist. No, not after years

of haunting, of your stepping just to the rim
of the snapshot, so that all I would see would be

a man's blurred silhouette half-cropped, crowded to the edge
by the messy plates on the table, the loaded fruit bowl; not
                                                    after years

of your appearing suddenly in a farther room, the library
or den, in someone else's apartment, to beckon, then vanish;

not after your trick of standing under the drizzled street lamp
late at night so the fauve green light underscored your eye
                                                    sockets

and the slash of your jaw. I see now: you were Krishna, you were
Apollo, provisionally. Then they departed.

According to their nature. And the elm near the crown of
                                        Peter's Hill
is left with out-flung branches—candelabra, octopus,

seaweed, lasso floating—still trying to embrace
the orbed horizon which eludes but dallies in its boughs.

Where they cut the longest branch last summer, the stump
still gestures out toward the sky beyond the sky.

Walking home, I see lime-yellow berries of pokeweed
glossing into purple. The park's blood is up,

it makes its offering: knobbed crab apples, crimson
hawthorn berries with their crinkled parchment leaves,

and the little scarlet cornucopias of deadly nightshade,
and weeping larch, and each rose of Sharon with its
                                    hemorrhage at heart,

and jewelweed, and small tough marigolds. As evening floats
                                                      down,
the train-rumble and traffic-wheeze tighten their cincture

around the hill, where the Japanese elm fingers a vanishing
                                          arc of shade.
You are not waiting, lounging against the stone gate of the park;

you are not standing by the lindens along the street.
Two urchins greet me there, a boy and girl, clambering on the
                                                        trunk

of someone's parked car. "We're just sliding," they explain.
Now they rappel up a municipal letterbox. The little boy

is dark, the girl elfin, blonde, her nostrils and upper lip
raw and brilliant from the feverish trickle of snot.

March Snow

Will it be gentle as this slow down-drifting
of the last flakes of winter, our separation?
The last one, I mean. The one we imagine
in a hospital room, with dim machines humming.
I hardly think so. Here outside my window
March wafts into extinction
as snow clumps melt from the roof and lapse
from boughs like loosened shawls falling.
All silent. The damp street steams.
This morning the house clamored with children
yanking brushes through hair, pulling on extra socks,
then suddenly the door slammed and out they went
into the soft, illusory drifts of early spring,
their lunch boxes swinging primary yellow and blue
against the belated white, small boots stamping a trail
that will melt into the future by late afternoon.

North

I.   Over Prairie

Not in but past
the piled tumultuous torsos we
hummed, silvering in our plane
safe on course and

belted to set directions: not
for us the heave
of shoulders, shudder of pectorals
and massed forearms where

Buonarroti's chisel bit
the confining strap, and tissue and muscle swelled;
not for us the pitching
cumulus thighs, braced buttocks, hips

squared in Titan cloudshock
where giants strove: we
stayed steady, we
held fast to cups and tray tables, only tremors

shook us—which we ignored—
while sidewise the sky lunged,
towered and seared its own
brainpans in spasm

after spasm of struck light. It's possible
to watch. It's possible not
to be taken, not to be
touched. It's possible to fly

not in, but past—

II.   The River

If it flashed a message in the pewtery twilight of northern
                                                  plains,
it was a wan one, about surfaces: how light does not adhere,
but adorns and momently describes as motionless a moving
                                                  current
and peels off into the minds of the beholders who stand,
                                    irresolute, on the bluff
watching the wild geese paddle steady in the wavering purl of
                                    weed by the little island,
and feel, already within them, the sheen this evening will hold
                                                  in memory
as the soiled water shrugs them off and moves away toward
                                                  night.

If you touch me, I will run through your hands like water.

III.   Home

Would it be ablution if the brook
clattered and lisped my prayers under its many tongues
and tumbled them down-

stream: would it shake
me free to have them swirl into the shadow where the
                                    mossbank hangs,
to let them shoot the rills, and run

from cascade to ambering eddy, beyond
heartshot, earshot, eyeshot? How absolved, if the heart keeps
                                    sloshing more
pleas forth from its dim

pump? Only if they blend
with the whole, choral tumult; how many prayers pour
each moment down this stream—

psalm of mountain, moose and fox
hunger, urine of bobcat, beaver, porcupine, deer; blood
of gashed trout in the otter's jaw:

and over the slickly mottled rocks
what curses, jokes, murmurs, what beer, spit, or sweat shed
from upstream? The brook will draw

no conclusions, deliver none:
in full foam-throttle, as now, or in drier, hoarse-throated spells,
it twines each private reverie to its own

and davens beyond our telling, what it tells.

August Walk

The forest fungal, and a seethe of rain.
Indian pipes prod white, crooked fingers up through mulch,
boletus and inky caps glutton in the dank.
Lichen glues coral to moist granite.
We follow cleft hoofprints
of a bull moose, you striding ahead, I lagging;
you reading woods-lore—ice-stripped bark, deer-nibble,
last winter's furry, matted fisher-cat spoor—; I distracted,
musing. The soil springs at our tread, mossbanks
bristle with spores. Rainlight shivers down.
The felled giant sugar maple has broken out
in boles: baroque, all bulging eyes,
beaks, foreheads, claws, diseased
and dark as a mahogany Roman choir stall.
Off the moose path now, it's an old farm you seek:
rock piles from last century's sheepfolds;
inward-lapsing cellar hole;
a tumble where the chimney stood;
at the threshold, by the granite doorslab,
a cluster of weed-choked lilies sprouted from lilies
the farm wife planted before the Civil War.
The road is a soft, Caesarean scar in tufted grass.
Each rain-glossed leaf emits a stab of green.
Somewhere, here, survives the idea of home.

Antique

It doesn't happen these days, the retinal shock when
one of them slips by, shoots

a glance, is gone—We were singed but
kept breathing. They don't

appear, after childhood. But
if he were to shiver into view, that

other one—lowercase kouros, lithe—
if he were to slide into sunlight here,

it would be on such a day: silver flakes
brisking in the woods as wind

whisks off mist and rainspatter, bark
ignites, birches sway: he can only step

from deepest shade. Do we have
darks enough to afford him

light? Over the pond, it's bronze, a Mycenaean
blade, black light smelted, that cleaves

sky from water, cirrus from leaf: he'd rise
from the gash, the core

of arterial night. He knows
the weight and lightness of a sword, how one flesh falls

from another, and both are true as he stands
in his gleam of rain, godsweat, oil. We know it

differently. By clasping—which is all we know
how, in our heaviness, to do—clasping

subtraction, and hearing it cry aloud, nightly, in our arms.

Eclogue

The high garden wall enclosed the corm
of the day, midday, and we sat together
on the wooden bench by the cypresses.
You had finished translating *The Phaedrus*.
High silence sheathed us. Beyond the wall,
carabinieri stood guard at another gate, and the city coughed.
"In order to speak justly," Socrates says,
"a man must labor through much practice
to adjust his words, not to men, but to the gods."
Scent of lavender drugged the air,
and that more bitter scent, of cypresses.
The carabinieri hold light machine guns, triggers cocked.
They look tired, young, bored. Socrates absorbed
several madnesses before he found his measure:
madness of the body's want, madness
of poetry, young men dangerous
with all their poetry springing from hips and loins.
How many nights, how many days,
have we looked for each other inside
the hurts we have made? Within the wall,
we say nothing, we have come far to sit on this volcanic hill
formed of ancient ashfall and boiling rivers of mud.
The city is built of rock, of blood, of mortared time.
The dialogue ends with Socrates'
prayer to Pan: for beauty within,

for harmony of inner and outer
self, for freedom from too much gold.
It is enough, this moment, not to speak. To touch your hand.

What Leaves

Evening congeals in the Forum but the story ambles
on behind columns, beyond the broken pedestal,
only a different story from the one we knew:

those figures are smaller, strolling over eons of mud,
than they suppose; an axe-blade of light
lops your shoulder from your spine, your head is absorbed

into the idea of an arch that has lost its bearings.
No one triumphs. No one's face is painted red.
If we are prisoners, it's in a private war

not chronicled in shadows clotting. The art
is all in not being becalmed, in a meal, in purchase,
in love: you are hunting a displaced person

who wandered off toward the vanishing point
but cracked and fell into the middle distance;
and if I follow, I'll be prying up shards

from this thickening pâté of dimness as it collects.
You leave a trail, but we are taken to pieces
into a story of processions, oratory, betrayal,

the severed head and hands impaled on the podium.
It's all in the giving up, as when, back on our hill,
the fountain pulses against a pelting rain

and rain strikes back into the fountain pool
and the fountain acknowledges the epic of water
and keeps spurting, from its aorta, its own small line.

For Trakl

Plocks of rain smite the sidewalk.
Evening tightens its hood, lowers its eyes.
The girl enters, shakes a shower
from heavy hair, turns, and passes

into an inner room. In the park, the pond shivers,
reflecting night into night. The path leads downhill.
Ilexes cringe where brother and sister met under the mass of
                                                        leaves.
Toads hop out around the fountain pool,

the satyr's blind marble eyes gleam.
A small body has been misplaced among the leaves, in sand.
Smoke taints the air, smoke and damp ash and the memory of
                                                        fire
where someone burned an ex-voto of a burned and blistering
                                                        hand.

Bonfires

(*Aeneid* XI)

Dawn had brought, meanwhile—always
the story happens mean-
while, during nights of sorrow and sore muscles, days
on the mountain cutting pine,

ash, cedar, oak—dawn had brought
light: dawn cracked the pitcher and
spilled that white-and-blue-sheen earliness out
over no-man's-land,

over ditches, stumps, tents, middens, and the tiresome
stacked dead, already foul.
Men in sogged light, moving, unmoving, a sum
gradually visible. To haul

one corpse, one foot, one line after another
onto the hacked logs—we
set stiff shoulders to stiffened limbs, pile fodder
onto pyres until we see

the spark catch and stack after stack go up
in black flame. And then the dizzy
circling of each fire, by custom, the tossing in of sword, cup,
helmet, bridle: easy,

repetitive once the flinging starts. Roman epic is painted
in black fire on black ground.
When the rhythm holds, anything burns on those canted
lines: oxen, swine, the stunned

still bleeding human victims, hands tied
behind their backs. The hero's
head aches, his lungs sear as he stands aside
and greasy smoke billows.

Fire by now has consumed an entire day.
Men wet earth and armor with tears.
Another tedious meanwhile is opening in the story.
Night comes on, distributing smutted stars.

Sicily

Itch, scabies, warts, burning, feces smeared in rags on the
                                                    sidewalk.
Isaac twists, blindfolded, on the altar under his father's knife.
Dawn polishes the silver blade of the sea's horizon.
The temple is poised on the hill crown with lightly folded
                                                    wings.
In a Moorish cloister, arches hang like lace. It has all
already happened: Jacob gripping the angel's thigh.
Lemons burn the tree. The tree still stands.
By morning, you will have wrested a blessing.
God raises his hand, he will use the blade to cut ocean from sky.
Isaac will walk, but he will always look behind him.
He will see gold and it will splinter in his eye.
The woman waits by the well; she will give birth to twins.
Twins will give birth to hate. Hate's wide womb will give birth
to Jacob gripping the angel's thigh
and to an explosion of gold in the firmament.
A synagogue stood here. Then a mosque.
For a blessing, grip firmly, twist, and apply pressure.
Pomegranates orbit in the vault.
The tree still stands. The baptismal font
is cracked and empty, and remembers where sunlight played.

Love Story

She lifts her right elbow straight up
like a spear thrust at heaven, though her hand trails down

behind her neck, groping for Artemis' invisible arrow.
She was shot from a distance and not by love

except in the sense that homicidal revenge betokens
love, in this case maternal, Leto's

passion to assert her supreme and pitiless
motherhood of twins. So other people's children

die, bewildered, this girl
a cascade of uncomprehending flesh

not quickened by any passion except
surprise. The volcano we saw

from a distance, across fields of Sicilian winter wheat,
shouldered into heaven, crowned with snow? with ash?

It loomed for two days, in and out of view,
fuming—source, witness, arbiter—seen now

through torch-licked smoke-stacks and billows of Siracusa's
refineries, now rearing white against the bullion

of lemon groves. The rented car
fled through the wide lap of fields

toward Enna and that feathery meadow where another girl
met love as earth spasmed and she fell through the crater

out of the known world, clutching a flower
with curling petals, like narcissus, sprung from a fat bulb.

Bonnard

It's like this: three large slices of
    world split into smaller, pulpy
        fistfuls of world within each

world-slice, and it all hurts, so
    debonair, so juicy: where
        is the woman, after all, the

center of this story? Well, we are
    mistaken. The center
        is a pillar of wrong

light, gone smooshed and overripe, re-
    flected, glassed, and we
        should be included but

we're not. It's not our house. The light
    doesn't smash us
        in the face or tilt

us backward out of our lives. Still,
    the column of garden
        hardly holds the story

together, and pomegranate seeds
    spill loose across the tiles and up
        the doorpost. So

many mirrors, you'd think, would give
    a point of view. They don't.
        They just ferment

sunlight into three species
    of jam. The seeds
        of light will stick

in our teeth, the paste of light
    wedge, unswallowed, in
        our throats. A flame

spurts in the toothy grate, but the soul
    stays dark. She's bent, the
        soul, steeped in her confiture

of shadows; leans naked, bruised,
    peripheral, half-
        erased. She's trying

to pray. She's trying to wash.
    She's shivering in
        cold. She has understood

that never, in this life, will she be clean.

Piazza Pilo

The low stone and stucco wall opens
    in gaps; you can pass

through, cross diagonally, or meander
    within; you can sit on one of

eight slatted benches under elms and read the paper, you
    can sit on the wall and chat or

listen to the radio if it's night and you're young, you can walk
    your dog: the park accepts

all, its pebbles crunch under business shoes as under
    sneakers ambling, the dog-walker's

loiter, trudge of an elderly woman laden
    with plastic grocery bags, the full-tilt

charge of one boy chasing
    another. If you're crippled

or retarded you can sit here and the elms
    don't rush their friendliness, they are

just poking into frowzy leaf, it's April, they
    seem happy to have you, so are the

old German shepherd and her terrier friend, so are
    the grayish men with newspapers: you

can throne in your wheelchair and take the sun, or hunch
    on the wall and mumble. The park

knows how to receive, how to
    let go. Its puddles sink

(it rained last night) slowly out of
    sight. If you're sick, aging, in love,

the park shows you how nightingales pelt out songs
    at dawn where last night's trash

spills from the corner basket. You could
    let someone kiss you, slowly:

you could open your mouth to surprise, a
    gift the gods

grant with other gifts: the staggering heart,
    ashes on the tongue, long patience at slow

breakage. Prayer. The word
    "unhealed." The word "farewell."

Lake

You stood thigh-deep in water and green light glanced
off your hip hollows and stomach which is where the pilot light
flickers in ancient statues of Dionysus,
and for a moment as you strode deeper it seemed as if
this water might rinse away the heaviness
of your own seasons and of illnesses not your own: it was a caress
cool and faithless, it lapped against your waist,
it took you in its arms and you gave yourself, a little,
only a little, knowing how soon and how lightly that touch
                                   would be withdrawn,
how soon you would be standing again on the rootwebbed
                                   shore, drying, restored
to the weights and measures, pulses, aches and scars you
                                   know by heart,
the cranky shoulder, cramping heel tendons, bad knees, bad
                                   dreams
you would recognize in the dark, anywhere, as your own;
and you knew, too, how those you cannot heal would remain
                                   unhealed
though you reach for them, kiss them on the forehead, and
                                   they stare back out of the drift;
and you knew the mountains would continue their slow,
                                   degrading shuffle to the sea
until continental plates shifted in their sleep, and this whole
                                   lake was swallowed
in earth's gasp, ocean's yawn.

Portrait: Marriage

Through the dark feathering of spruce boughs and crosshatch
      of naked lower branches, through
splatters of beechlight and beyond the shuddered patch
of sky trapped in the pond's net of depth and shade,
      you flicker into view
      a moment, then subside

into mingled inks and umbers, like the paper birch
      reflected: shaft of brilliance probing
the pond's amnesia: whole: fractured at a touch:
that's how I've seen you over the years,
      light robing and disrobing
      an image upon shaken waters;

that's how I've held you, as one embraces and loses
      the muscled slide of water in mid-
stroke, cold, hauling forward to new darkness as
it passes. Now, almost invisible at the pond's edge,
      you rake years of mud,
      leafmire, twiggy sludge,

and pitch it into the barrow where I hear the clank
        of tines on metal lip, the lurch
as you trundle it back to mulch the iris bank.
Time, Lord knows, has many bodies, and we learn
        slowly enough: dredge
        of mortal muck, burn

of sunlight on birchbark and, more shiftingly, on
        the reflected birch. Here, you're back: flash
of ripped white T-shirt, a holler. Yes, I'll come down
and keep you company. I want to feel
        you for a moment—slapdash,
        sweaty, whole—

as the woods hang back from us. Let's make this scar
        in chiaroscuro, in the leaflit air,
let's leave traces in the fibrous soil where we are
standing for now, since now is a proposition
        molded over and over
        in water, loam, and stone.

Notes

"Cassandra": "Wherever the splendid sun beats down on sorrow" translates a line in Italian from Ugo Foscolo's monumental poem, "Dei Sepolcri."

"Poetry Reading": This poem was composed on the occasion of the First Inauguration of President Clinton, and was printed, with other poems inspired by that event, in *The Washington Post*, December 13, 1992. In echoing Virgil's lament for Marcellus, the nephew of Augustus and his son-in-law and heir, the poem remembers the scene of Virgil's reading Book VI of *The Aeneid* aloud to the emperor and his court. Hearing the lines about her son Marcellus, Augustus's sister Octavia fainted.

"'Departure'": The title comes from Max Beckmann's triptych in the Museum of Modern Art in New York. The poem splices quotations from the Italian poet Guido Guinizelli (1240?–?1274) and from Beckmann (1884–1950). The lines I have translated from

Guinizelli come from his "Al cor gentil rempaira sempre Amore";
the lines from Beckmann are adapted from remarks recorded in
Max Beckmann's Triptychs by Charles S. Kessler (Cambridge: Har-
vard University Press, 1970).

"L'Oiseau de nuit": The last stanza translates and sets to verse
a sentence from Colette's story, "Où sont les enfants?" from *La
Maison de Claudine*.

"Intimate Letters": The title comes from one of Janáček's last
works, the String Quartet Number 2 (1928). The poem quotes
extensively from, and rearranges, sentences in the correspondence
of the composer Leoš Janáček and Kamila Stösslová, a young mar-
ried woman whom he met at the Moravian spa town of Luhačovice
in 1917. Janáček was sixty-three when they met, Kamila Stösslová
twenty-five. She was a conventional young woman, poorly edu-
cated, and fully (and, it appears happily) occupied in her marriage
to David Stössel, a dealer in antiques and paintings. The couple
had two boys, Rudolf (born 1913) and Otto (born 1916). Janáček,
who had been estranged from his wife, Zdenka Janáčková, for many
years, though they still lived together in the city of Brno, became
enamored of Kamila. For the last eleven years of his life, she was his
muse and his passion, inspiring many of his late works. As the let-
ters show, this love developed mainly through distance and separa-
tion, as Mrs. Stösslová stayed loyal to her husband and would
permit no physical impropriety, though she and her husband did
occasionally visit the Janáčeks, and though Janáček did visit them,
off and on, in the town of Písek where they lived. In the last few
days of the composer's life, Kamila finally came to spend a few days
with him in his summer cottage in his boyhood village, Hukvaldy,
with her son Otto. It was there that Janáček caught the pneumonia
that killed him.

The story is told through the selection of letters, *Intimate Letters*, beautifully edited and translated by John Tyrrell (Princeton: Princeton University Press, 1994). The lines I have quoted come from that book and also from *Janáček: Leaves from His Life*, edited and translated by Vilem and Margaret Tausky (New York: Taplinger, 1982), and from *Leos Janáček* by Ian Horsbrugh (New York: Scribners, 1981). Zdenka Janáčková, Janáček's widow, gives her own version of the story in *My Life with Janáček*, edited and translated by John Tyrrell (London and Boston: Faber and Faber, 1998).

Janáček used to jot down words he heard in conversation, and set them to music. I have tried to arrange the words of Janáček and Mrs. Stösslová as a kind of poetic score, responsive to qualities I hear in the string quartet he wrote for her.

I have abbreviated book titles as follows: *Intimate Letters* as IL, *Janáček: Leaves from His Life* as *Leaves*; and *Leoš Janáček* as LJ.

"when she tosses her head like that . . ." IL 134.

"Two decidedly Jewish types . . ." IL 7.

"a fine of ten crowns . . ." *Leaves* 66.

"She was of medium height . . ." IL 7.

"her raven hair, all loose . . ." IL 48

"And your eye has a strange depth . . ." IL 48.

"the chord of stalagmites covered with hoarfrost . . ." *Leaves* 70.

Olga's dying words are transcribed from Janáček's notebook page, reproduced in LJ 52.

"The rivers of Lachia . . ." *Leaves* 30.

"Where is the poet Šťastný . . ." *Leaves* 30.

"So it's like a stone falling into water . . ." IL 23.

"You're the star I look for in the evening . . ." IL 39.

"There's no love just innocent friendship . . ." IL39.

"I was your shadow . . ." IL 103.

"Even thoughts become flesh . . ." IL 104.

"I'm really an ordinary woman . . ." IL 50.

"For that cold . . ." IL 164.

"like an exhausted little bird . . ." IL 3.

"Dear Madam, Accept these few roses . . ." IL 3.

"Silence goes to sleep under every tree . . ." IL 22.

"your little hand . . ." IL 127.

". . . were written in fire . . ." IL 282.

"Zdenka must understand . . ." adapted from the letter of June 8, 1927, IL 121.

"I want to have the painting . . ." IL 225.

"And I kissed you . . ." Janáček's last entry in the album he shared with Kamila, a day or so before his death. IL 344.

"From the Notebooks of Anne Verveine": Anne Verveine is an imaginary French poet. She was born in 1965 in the village of Magagnosc in the Alpes Maritimes, and attended the *lycée* in Grasse. She never studied at a university. She lived obscurely in Paris, avoiding literary society and working as a typographer and designer for a small publisher of art books. She published a few poems in provincial journals, but no book of her own work. She was last seen hitchhiking in Uzbekistan in August 2000; is presumed kidnapped or dead.

Anne Verveine's sister found these poems in notebooks in the poet's small apartment in Paris after her disappearance. I translate them.

"What Leaves": This poem bears in mind Cicero's assassination in 43 B.C.E. and the exhibition of his head on a spike on the rostrum in the Forum where he had given so many speeches. Lincoln Perry's paintings of the Forum helped to prompt the poem.